FORESTS and WOODLANDS

Rose Pipes

A ZOË BOOK

A ZOË BOOK

© 1998 Zoë Books Limited

Devised and produced by
Zoë Books Limited
15 Worthy Lane
Winchester
Hampshire SO23 7AB
England

First published in Great Britain in 1998 by
Zoë Books Limited
15 Worthy Lane
Winchester
Hampshire SO23 7AB

A record of the CIP data is available from the British Library.

ISBN 1 86173 019 5

Printed in Hong Kong by Midas Printing Ltd.
Editor: Kath Davies
Map: Sterling Associates
Design & Production: Sterling Associates

Photographic acknowledgments

The publishers wish to acknowledge, with thanks, the following photographic sources:

Environmental Images / Irene Lengui 22; / Chris Martin 25; The Hutchison Library / Andrey Zvoznikov 14; / Edward Parker 23; / Nick Owen 29; Impact Photos / Jonathan Pile 27; NHPA / David Woodfall - cover inset bl, 5; / John Shaw 13; / Michael Leach 15; / A.N.T. 19, 21; / Andy Rouse 28; South American Pictures / Chris Sharp - title page; Still Pictures / Francois Pierrel - cover inset tr; / Bruno Cavignaux 7; / Clyde H.Smith 9; / Roland Sietre 16; / Mark Edwards 20; / Thomas Raupach 24; / Michel Gunther 26; TRIP / R.Surman - cover background; / P.Rauter 8; / Viesti Associates © Stephen G.Maka 10; / W.Fraser 12; Woodfall Wild Images / David Woodfall 6; / Lisa Husar 11; / M.Biancarelli 17; / Ted Mead 18.

The publishers have made every effort to trace the copyright holders, but if they have inadvertently overlooked any, they will be pleased to make the necessary arrangement at the first opportunity.

Contents

Where do forests and woodlands grow?   4

Wildlife in forests and woodlands   6

Using forest trees   8

North America's mixed woodlands   10

Russia's coniferous forests   14

Australia's eucalyptus woodlands   18

Mangrove forests in Central and
    South America   22

Bamboo forests in China   26

Glossary   30

Index   32

Where do forests and woodlands grow?

Trees need a lot of water, so forests and woodlands grow in places where plenty of rain falls.

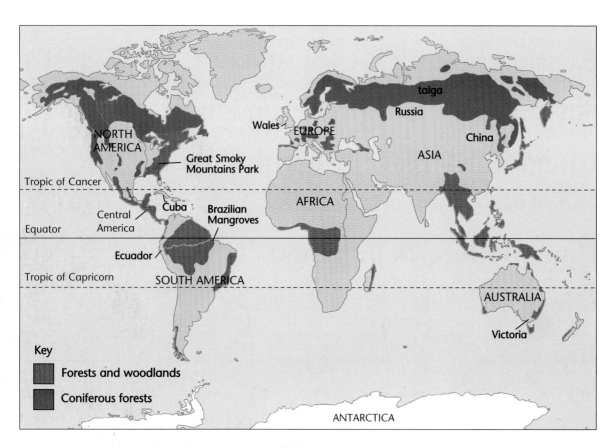

Here are the world's largest forests and woodlands. The ones you will read about are named on this map.

Coniferous trees can grow in places where winters are long and cold. Most coniferous trees have green, needle-shaped leaves all year. They are **evergreen** trees.

Deciduous trees have flat leaves that change colour and drop in the autumn. Deciduous woodlands grow in milder, wetter places than coniferous forests.

There are deciduous and coniferous trees in this woodland in Wales.

Wildlife in forests and woodlands

Thick, coniferous forests are too dark for flowers to grow.

In open, deciduous woodlands, sunlight can reach the ground below the trees. Wild flowers, like these bluebells, grow there.

Trees provide food as well as homes for birds and other animals. Animals eat the nuts, fruits, leaves, seeds and bark from trees, and make nests in tree trunks or branches.

Most forest animals are **adapted** to living in trees. This red squirrel has sharp claws to help it to climb. The squirrel also has strong, sharp teeth that can crack open hard nuts.

Using forest trees

We use wood to make buildings, furniture and many other things. Nuts, fruits, leaves, oils and **sap** from trees also have uses. Some can be eaten, or used to make medicines.

These trees are felled for their wood, or timber.

Cutting down trees destroys **habitats**. In many countries there are now special parks and nature **reserves**. Here, the trees and the wildlife are **protected**.

In northern lands, **acid rain** has killed many trees. The rain picks up gases from factory smoke, cars and trucks. It poisons, or **pollutes**, the trees when it falls on them.

These dead trees are in the Blue Ridge Mountains in the United States of America (USA). Acid rain killed them.

North America's mixed woodlands

Mixed woodlands grow in the central and eastern States of North America. The trees are mostly deciduous, such as hickories,

These beautiful woodlands are in Maine, USA.

maples and oaks, but evergreen pines also grow there. There are towns, roads and cities in North America's woodlands.

Many woodland animals are now **extinct**. They died out because they lost their habitats, or were hunted.

Other animals, such as raccoons and bob cats, survived. They have adapted to town life.

Before towns were built, raccoons always lived in trees and ate wild foods. Many raccoons now eat garbage and live inside empty buildings.

The sugar maple tree produces sap which people make into sugar and syrup. One large tree can produce about two kilogrammes of sugar. The sugar maple is now in danger from acid rain.

Some woodlands are protected in **National Parks**. One of these Parks is

The buckets on these trees collect sap to make into syrup.

the Great Smoky Mountains Park. Many different trees grow here, such as oaks, hemlocks and pines. There are more than 1000 kinds of plant, and small trees and shrubs with beautiful blossoms. The rare yellow lady's slipper grows here, too.

Wild turkeys and bears live among the trees. Turkeys eat nuts and seeds.

Springtime in the Great Smoky Mountains Park in the Appalachian Mountains

Russia's coniferous forests

The largest forest in the world grows across northern Russia. It is known as the **taiga**.

Winters in the taiga are very long, cold and snowy.

The forest is home to many wild animals. The lynx is one of the largest forest **mammals**. The largest bird is the capercaillie.

Capercaillies eat conifer shoots and tree needles. Smaller crossbills eat seeds from the woody cones of the conifers.

Crossbills use their crossed bills to open the cones and their long tongues to reach the seeds.

Timber from taiga trees is made into wood pulp and paper at paper mills. Russia **exports** a large amount of timber and paper.

This paper mill is beside Lake Baikal in Russia. The lake is badly polluted by chemicals from mills like this one.

Small parts of the taiga are protected in reserves. Outside the reserves, wild animals are in danger from hunting.

Wildlife habitats are destroyed by forest fires and pollution, and when people flood the land to make **reservoirs**.

Animals such as the sable and this lynx are in danger from hunting and loss of habitat.

Australia's eucalyptus woodlands

Eucalyptus trees are called gum trees in Australia. Some gum trees grow as tall as 90 metres.

This eucalyptus woodland is in the State of Victoria, in southern Australia.

The possum lives in eucalyptus woodlands. There are many kinds of possum, and some of them are **gliders**.

Possums feed on the leaves, buds and shoots of gum trees. The sugar glider possum lives in hollows in the tree trunks.

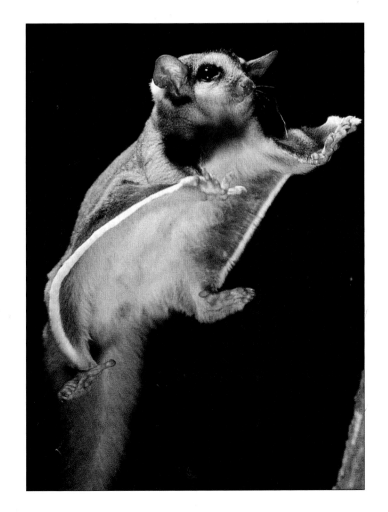

The skin between the front and back legs of gliders stretches out to form wings. When the animal jumps from a tree, it can glide across to another tree more than 100 metres away.

The leaves of gum trees contain a strong-scented oil. This oil, and the gum in the trees, makes the trees burn very easily.

Forest fires often happen in the eucalyptus woodlands. But the trees are well adapted to fire. After a tree is burnt, buds below the bark grow very quickly.

People use gum wood in many ways, such as for fuel, for building and for making fences. The bark is used in leather-making, and to make paper.

Eucalyptus woodlands provide habitats for wild animals such as the koala.

Koalas eat the leaves of gum trees and make their homes in the branches.

Mangrove forests in Central and South America

Mangrove trees grow around the coasts of most **tropical** countries. They grow on flat

These mangroves are on the coast of Brazil, a country in South America.

land which sea water covers when the **tide** comes in. Many kinds of mangrove tree grow in tropical South and Central America. Some are 40-50 metres tall, others only one metre.

Mangroves are well adapted to their coastal habitat. They have long roots called prop roots to hold them firmly in the mud.

Some kinds of mangrove also have tiny, pencil-thin roots that grow up above the water. These help the trees to take in air. You can see both kinds of root in the photograph.

People who live in the forests use the mangrove wood as fuel. In some places, people try to preserve the trees by cutting off branches instead of felling whole trees. This helps to protect the forest habitat.

In Cuba, there are crocodile farms in the mangrove forests. Tourists often visit the farms.

People sometimes clear away the forest to make boating **marinas** to attract tourists. In some places, farmers have also cleared trees away to use the land for shrimp ponds. The farmers catch and sell the shrimps.

Mangrove trees have been cut down to make space for this shrimp farm in Ecuador.

Bamboo forests in China

Bamboo is a tree-like grass that can grow as tall as 20 metres.

In the mountains of western China, bamboo grows in clumps, or thickets, in the forests.

Bamboo is strong and can bend without breaking. People use it to make scaffolding and ladders. There are bamboo musical instruments and furniture. Split bamboo is woven into mats and made into chopsticks.

Bamboo scaffolding on buildings in Hong Kong

China's pandas live in bamboo thickets in the mountain forests. Bamboo is their main food.

A sixth finger on their front paws helps pandas to hold the bamboo while they eat it.

People cut down bamboo forests to make farmland. The pandas who used to live there are dying out because their habitat is being destroyed.

There are only about 800 pandas left in China. Now they live in forest reserves where they are protected.

Farms in the countryside near Dali, where the bamboo forest has been cleared.

Glossary

acid rain: rain which contains acid from car and truck exhausts.

adapted: if a plant or an animal can find everything it needs to live in a place, we say it has adapted to that place. The animals can find food and shelter, and the plants have enough food in the soil and enough water. Some animals have changed their shape or their colour over a long time, so that they can catch food or hide easily. Some plants in dry areas can store water in their stems or roots.

coniferous: trees that have cones and needle-shaped leaves.

deciduous: trees that usually have broad leaves which change colour and fall off in the autumn.

exports: goods that are sold and taken to other countries.

extinct: a kind of animal which has died out.

evergreen: trees that have green leaves all year round.

gliders: animals which can glide from tree to tree by stretching out their skin to form wings.

habitat: the natural home of a plant or animal. Examples of habitats are deserts, forests and wetlands.

mammals: a group of animals whose young feed on their mother's milk.

marinas: places where boats are moored. There are often wooden walkways above the water, leading to the boats.

National Parks: laws protect these lands and their wildlife from harm. These places usually have beautiful scenery and rare wildlife.

pollutes: dirties or poisons.

protected: kept safe from changes that damage the wildlife or habitat.

reserves: areas set aside for wildlife to live in safely.

reservoirs: lakes which have been specially made to store water for people to use.

sap: a liquid, or juice, made inside trees.

taiga: the Russian word for a dark, mysterious woodland.

tide: the rising and falling of the level of the sea each day.

tropical: places that are hot and wet all year are called tropical. They are close to the Tropics (shown on the map on page 4).

Index

acid rain 9, 12
animals 7, 11, 13, 15, 17, 19, 21
Australia 18, 19, 20, 21

Baikal, Lake 16
bamboo 26, 27, 28, 29
birds 7, 13, 15
Brazil 22

Central America 22, 23
China 26, 27, 28, 29
coniferous trees 5, 6, 14, 15
Cuba 24

deciduous trees 5, 6, 10

Ecuador 25
evergreen trees 5, 11

farms 24, 25, 29
food 7, 11, 19, 21, 28
forest fires 17, 20
fuel 21, 24

habitats 9, 11, 17, 23, 24, 29
Hong Kong 27
hunting 11, 17

koala 21

lynx 15, 17

mammals 15
mangrove trees 22, 23, 24, 25
mills 16

National Parks 12, 13

pandas 28, 29
paper 16, 21
plants 13
pollution 9, 16, 17
possum 19

raccoons 11
reserves 9, 17
reservoirs 17
Russia 14, 15, 16, 17

South America 22, 23
sugar maples 12

taiga 14, 17
timber 8, 16
tourists 24, 25

United States of America (USA) 9, 10, 11, 12, 13

Wales 5
wildlife 6, 7, 8, 9, 17